Riding with Oliveira

also by Dominique Barbier

The Alchemy of Lightness (with Dr. Maria Katsamanis)

Meditation for Two (with Keron Psillas)

Dressage for the New Age

Riding with Oliveira

My Time with the Mestre—Forty Years Later

Dominique Barbier & Keron Psillas

Foreword by *Maria da Pureza Oliveira*

TRAFALGAR SQUARE
North Pomfret, Vermont

First published in 2018 by
Trafalgar Square Books
North Pomfret, Vermont 05053

Library of Congress Cataloging-in-Publication Data
Names: Barbier, Dominique, 1950- author. | Psillas, Keron, photographer.
Title: Riding with Oliveira : my time with the Mestre--forty years later /
  Dominique Barbier & Keron Psillas.
Description: North Pomfret, Vermont : Trafalgar Square Books, 2018.
Identifiers: LCCN 2018019736| ISBN 9781570768835 (hardcover) | ISBN
  9781570769252 (ebook)
Subjects: LCSH: Barbier, Dominique, 1950- | Oliviera, Nuno, 1925-1989. |
  Dressage horse trainers--Biography. | Dressage. | Horsemanship. | LCGFT:
  Autobiographies.
Classification: LCC SF309.482.B37 A3 2018 | DDC 798.2/3092 [B] --dc23
LC record available at https://lccn.loc.gov/2018019736

Book design by *Katarzyna Misiukanis–Celińska*
Cover design by *RM Didier*
Index by *Michelle A. Guiliano (linebylineindexing.com)*
Typefaces: Book Antiqua, Baskerville Old Face and Candlescript Pro

Printed in China

10 9 8 7 6 5 4 3 2 1

dedication.

for my father,

Pierre Barbier,

who sensed my deep dedication and allowed me
to pursue what became my life's work — to love
and understand horses.

and for the

Société pour L'Art Equestre,

which has been created by people who want to help horses
in this very confused world and to give back to horses
the gift of healing that they have so freely given to us.

contents.

foreword.

My memories of Dominique Barbier intertwine and flow together: I am slowly walking through a shady, silent corridor; a fluid wall slides along, a screen of black trees and sudden brightness passes by, and as I touch it, there is a glimpse of a smile, golden hair, followed by two light blue eyes. And now the trees disappear behind a huge golden mustache...then the mustache, the blue eyes, and the curly golden hair disappear under the ocean and come back up laughing, glittering under the morning sun. Now the ocean is gone, and I see this young man riding a gray horse into the hills, and disappearing behind the solitary stone houses, whistling like a bird. And those trees fade into a misty gray morning, where again, there he is, far away, running with a little black-and-white dog near the surf. The white foam transforms into a small, light-colored car, its engine dying at sunset in the middle of a hay field that leads nowhere after faithfully performing millions of dangerous circles on roundabouts while its owner laughs like crazy.

And I remember…I remember who he is…a young man with an enormous thirst for life and happiness, and who would go to hell and heaven just to have a taste of it.

This is the young man who came and studied the equestrian art with my father, Nuno Oliveira.

Let me share the history of my father's origins, as perhaps it will help you understand him.

His father—my grandfather—became a pastor after retiring from a very good position in the international department of an important bank in Lisbon. He was also an erudite with a big library of books on comparative religion, philosophy, and ancient history. He transcribed the Bible into modern Portuguese, gave regular speeches abroad on Christianity, and wrote research books on the same subject. He also maintained an active epistolary exchange with pastors and priests of various factions of Christianity within several countries.

My grandfather was the son of a very interesting couple: My great-grandfather was a Navy commander of a ship and honored by the King for his feats. My great-grandmother was a person of culture and talent who exchanged correspondence with known writers and artists and painted very well, spoke six languages, and kept an impressive library of her own. She introduced my grandfather to classical music. *Her* grandfather, António de Oliveira Marreca, was a mason, eminent economist, and a writer, and he is still studied today. He was a deputy in the parliament and fought along with other well-known intellectuals in the movement that later led to the implementation of the Portuguese Republic—his statue stands in Santarém, where he was born.

My father's mother was the daughter of a Galician Lady who was closely related by blood to the Countess Emilia Pardo Bázan, a prolific writer, who is still revered today and whose statue stands in La Corunã, Galicia. My grandmother's father was a wealthy industrialist, honored by King Dom Manuel II in documents my family possesses. My great-grandparents took their five children to London, following the King's exile there after the 1910 revolution and dissolution of the monarchy. They remained in England for fifteen years.

▲ *Maria Pureza Oliveira on Don Juan, 1976.*

Allow me to share one family story: Besides having a private train suite
in the international train (that could be separated from other carriages),
similar to that of the King, my great-grandfather bought a yacht from him
called the *Chalupa Maria*. One day when he and his family came ashore
in Cascais for dinner, the boat was sunk as the crew had become drunk
before a storm arrived. The royal tableware my great-grandfather had
also bought—together with the ship—was floating in the bay of Cascais,
and the yacht was completely wrecked!

My father's own *mestre*, his cousin, was the *Picador da Casa Real*,
the Teacher of the King.

As it has been noted by many others, my father was proud (and rightly
so) and an acutely sensitive person. He was extremely humiliated by
the pedantic attitudes of some people among the Portuguese high society,
who, either due to intellectual poverty, class malformation, or envy of
his extraordinary talent, looked upon him the same way the nobles used
to look upon their musicians (Handel, Beethoven, Mozart, and so on) as
mean servants. Of course, nowadays, we consider these artists geniuses.

My father did not feel inferior, and so he was hurt by people
"inferiorizing" him — people who could do so only because they had
high positions, not because they had high intellectual or moral status.
I am of course talking about only some people in society, not all,
and we know that very noble (in all senses of the word) friends of his
supported and understood him throughout his life. He always privately
and publicly acknowledged their kindness and friendship. ▪

Maria Pureza Oliveira, Avessada

ALTHOUGH FADED BY TIME, THIS PHOTOGRAPH
STILL BEARS THE MARKS OF THE MESTRE'S HAND.
It reads: For Monsieur Barbier, with my admiration, Nuno Oliveira.

DOMINIQUE BARBIER

in the picadeiro at Quinta do Brejo, the arena where Dominique learned from Mestre Nuno Oliveira, in September 2013.

introduction.

Master, *mestre*, guru, teacher…these are important words. The true *mestre* is a person who directs and changes your life. The guru is a person who dissipates the darkness by showing you the light. I have lived my life between the two worlds—the one we *see*, which is limited (the illusion) and the one we *feel*, which is unlimited.

I always felt *The Mestre, my Mestre*, Nuno Waldemar Nuñez Marques Cardoso Pery-de-Linde Marreca de Abreu Oliveira —the revered Portuguese equestrian who inspired others all over the world to explore the "classical" style of working with the horse—existed between two worlds, as well.

I believe he had a great gift and an important mission. He was misunderstood and sometimes ridiculed. But I know he had something that no one else had: a deep understanding of his art. Through great discipline, scholarly, serious inquiry and analysis, and a nonstop relentless passion, he formed his understanding of the equestrian art. He was more French than most French people in many ways…he read and understood more books

When I first saw the Mestre, I realized there was another world with horses… some sort of secret, nearly unattainable world (for me and most of us) that he navigated with ease. But I always thought it just within reach if I was open to learning.

than all of us and was able to communicate with deeply intellectual people, like equestrian scholar and philosopher René Bacharach, who translated the Mestre's first book *Reflections on Equestrian Art* from Portuguese to French. But there existed, at the same time, a man that lived apart from all of this. A man who lived with an intensity rarely seen. This passion, this fire, along with his extraordinary knowledge, was what attracted the best riding students to him.

understated man I know, Luis has lived a life that shows hard work and dedication will bring you great success. He would say that his success is evident in three things, in this order: his family, his horses, his work.

I posed the same questions to each of my friends:
- *When did you meet the Mestre?*
- *What did you feel at that moment?*
- *How did his teaching affect you? And how did your riding, and the way you think about riding, change?*
- *How did Mestre Oliveira's teaching mature in your life over the years?*
- *How does it resonate today in your horses, in your everyday teaching, and in you?*

It is my hope and belief that when you read the answers to their questions you will perhaps find answers to questions of your own. I have left their testimony as it was offered to me — unfiltered. As each of us is an individual, and everyone has his or her own perceptions and feelings, their responses ranged from the deeply personal to the technical, to the specific acts that illustrate an equestrian life that was lived in a passionate way.

We are always talking about ourselves. We are, after all, just mirrors for each other. But Mestre Nuno Oliveira was an extraordinary mirror. There was nothing mundane, banal, small in his reflection. Those things were burned away by his brilliance. We were all better for it. ■

without aggression, to love without condition, and to avoid the destructive side of perfection.

beginnings.

I was born in France in 1950, and it was while at a Jesuit school in Poitiers that I discovered horses were my calling. At the age of fifteen, I attended Crabbett Park Equestrian Centre in West Sussex, England, and I would return to England in my twenties to attend the renowned Talland School of Equitation in Cirencester before exploring horsemanship and various disciplines—including show jumping, eventing, dressage, and steeplechase—at a number of highly regarded facilities throughout Europe.

At some point I knew that I wanted to finish my equestrian education with Mestre Nuno Oliveira in Portugal. For all the time I was in England, I dreamed of it. Everyone said he was the man to be with, who taught in the style in which I already knew I wanted to learn — that of the Baroque or classical way, based on the teachings of great riding masters such as François Robichon de La Guérinière, Gustav Steinbrecht, and François Baucher. This was during the time the Mestre went to the renowned *Cadre Noir* in Saumur, France — the first foreign *écuyer* (riding instructor) to be invited to teach there.

In Portugal, I discovered that the Mestre did not have fond memories of the British influence early in his life so my having trained so long in England was not a "plus." He said to me, "Ah! You come from England!" I was twenty-two; the Mestre was forty-seven. I was young and unknown; he was famous worldwide and very impressive. And there I was, too properly dressed, and the Mestre said to me sarcastically, "I like your British jacket."

I arrived in Portugal in the winter. As residents of a southern European country, the Portuguese pretend that winter does not exist. The houses are not built for winter, nor the rains that come in January and the damp and cold that sets into the stone and masonry and stays until May! I found a place to live in Póvoa Santo Adrião — a room in a small apartment owned by a British couple. It was basic and good. I remember fondly their sweetness and desire to be helpful.

//cold mornings.

Learning that the Mestre started riding at half past four each morning, of course I went the very first day. The wooden stairs up to the gallery overlooking the *picadeiro* squeaked, and the door was even worse.

▲ *The Mestre at home in the picadeiro.*

There was no way to be invisible. I will remember all my life the big eyes he turned on me—a mixture of, "What are you doing?" and "I am happy someone is here." He loved an audience, and I can relate to that.

At 11:00 a.m. the students rode, then we had lunch, then the Mestre rode three more horses in the afternoon, after which we had a group lesson. But my favorite time by far was half past four in the morning, cold, silent, and alone. Just the Mestre, a horse, and me in a very small place. It was delicious.

I could not wait for each morning. Watching Mestre Oliveira was surreal. He was a big man. Meeting him in the street you could not know that he was the finest *écuyer* in the world. He reminded me of Jean-Pierre Rampal, the famous French flautist—a very large man playing the lightest flute in the world. Oliveira's teaching was minimal and personally given. Watching was the only way for me to absorb all I craved to know… watching him over and over again. I recall living (and learning) by *being* him many times over. Not watching but *being* him. Riding and living through him almost "molecularly."

This instinct was so strong it fascinated me. Many times I thought about it and concentrated on making it work for me even better. The more I practiced this technique of watching and learning by *being*, the sooner I found refinement of my objective—improvement of my ability on horseback. Over the years I have developed many techniques based on this understanding and practice. My hours and hours of watching the Mestre at work have become even more important to me, if that is possible. Then I was absolutely intent on observing and using every nuance I could discern. And the more I watched that big man on a horse, the more I saw, and the more I felt. And the more I felt, the more I could transmit to my own horses.

Ten days after my arrival in Póvoa de Santo Adrião, the Mestre gave me the experience of my life. It was early in the morning, and I had my notebook in my pocket (what would one day become my book *Dressage for the New Age*). The Mestre was riding a great big gray horse belonging to a banker. The horse had sinking hips because of an accident early in his life, and only the Mestre rode him. Halfway through the session he stopped and called out, looking up at me, alone in the gallery, "You! Come down! "

My heart was pounding as I very quickly went down the creaky stairs in my street clothes: English jacket (you cannot ride without it in England) and Italian shoes. He asked me to mount the gray and canter on the circle to the right. You must understand, the *picadeiro* was very small, just the size of two longeing circles. So this horse was cantering around, and the Mestre said, *"Descente de main, descente de jambes."*

I knew: lower my hands and legs. Then he said, "Reins at the buckle." I could do that, too. Next he instructed: "Lengthen the canter down the long side and circle again." I loosened my back to lengthen the stride and the horse lengthened five or six strides. But then he announced, "Collect your horse! "

The gray was already going too fast and I had no contact with his mouth; therefore, I instinctually went to pick up the reins.

reflections.

"Barbier! You are too simple!"
Mestre Oliveira would say.
*"Thank you, Mestre, thank you, Mestre!
You are too kind!"* I would reply.

I confess I try always to return to simplicity.
To simplify without losing the intent, to make it more
palatable and understandable for the horses
and the riders. Horses are very simple creatures
but creatures with an enormous capacity for teaching us.
Teaching us what? How they want to be ridden,
how we can do more with doing much less,
how we can bring compassion to every action.
Quite simply: how to live. My Mestre, along with my horses,
created the foundation for the life
I have built. It is that simple.

ENRIQUE BARBIER

on Sargento Do Top.

"Oh no!" the Mestre bellowed.

Panic! What should I do?

I thought about leaning back and "growing taller" in the saddle, and as I did I felt that incredible moment when the big horse came back to me, just with my brain sending him an image and my back growing taller. He rounded and collected beneath me *without* the reins. It was the epiphany of my life. I knew at that moment what I wanted to do with my horses and what I had to teach to others. It was a very powerful lesson.

Mestre Oliveira told me to dismount and that was it. But it was one very early morning in Portugal that has never been forgotten and instead formed the very foundation for my riding and teaching in my lifetime ahead.

//how life prepared me for the mestre.

When I was seven years old we lived in a little town in southwestern France called Cognac. My parents had a high-end deli-grocery that would create my taste for food for the rest of my life. It ruined me, really. Chocolate, truffles, foie gras—the best of everything.

Anyway, I was a sickly child. My father was dedicated to making me stronger and more confident. My brother and I began to study judo. My teacher Mr. Durand was seventy years old and the only Westerner to achieve the rank of 7-dan, based on the system out of 10 formed in Japan. A higher dan indicates more leadership ability, teaching experience, and service to the art. I could not have had a better beginning to the discipline.

early days in póvoa de santo adrião.

AS I mentioned at the beginning of this book, I believe Mestre Nuno Oliveira had a great gift and a very important mission. Additionally, he was able to motivate his disciples to change their lives and to apply themselves to a similar mission.

At the beginning of his life it was difficult for the Mestre to prove himself in the very specialized world of Portuguese equitation. He was very strong and efficient. Later in his life we saw more mental work—"Less technique, more love,"

▲ *The Mestre on Soante in his "laboratory."*

he used to say. But he often had a difficult time. He felt deficient in the modern world (for example, he never drove an automobile). Oliveira's background in this way was much like the French riding master François Baucher's. He was misunderstood and sometimes treated with contempt.

Frenchman and renowned rider and trainer in the classical tradition Michel Henriquet was a great support at the beginning of Oliveira's life. Through their friendship and letters, they helped each other. Henriquet wanted to know what was happening in Portugal with French classical dressage (as basically not much was going on in France at that time) and Oliveira was analyzing and discovering in the *picadeiro* ("working in his laboratory," as my friend Mestre Luis Valença aptly described it), then communicating ideas with his friend. This served as a kind of validation, I believe. It gave a structure that was necessary for him to continue this search; to understand classical French riding and support the refinement of his own method throughout the rest of his life.

//revolution.

My first period in Portugal was the time just before and during the Carnation Revolution of 1974. This bloodless coup ended the Salazar Estado Novo regime—the longest dictatorship in twentieth century Europe. This was an event that changed many things in Portugal and in Mestre Oliveira's life. Portugal had been a very under-control country, and then suddenly, almost the next day, there was massive disorganization. Everyone was very disturbed, not knowing what was happening, who was going to rule, and how they would lead.

Before the Revolution, there was a great deal of fear all over the country. Lack of food, lack of money…it was a difficult time. People had trouble taking care of horses.

I remember there was a big property on one side of the Rio Tejo (the longest river on the Iberian Peninsula) that was used by the public for recreation and for hunting. But then one day the property was entirely enclosed with a big fence. Who was in charge? No one knew the answer. These kinds of incidents were what started the Revolution. The targets of anger and frustration were the rich people who did not use their land. Five hundred people owned almost all of Portugal, and many, many farms were not being used. The Mestre felt afraid, as many did, during this time, but in reality nothing was going to happen to him because he was not a target—he was not part of the landed gentry or nobility.

//the mestre's ability.

I believe that Oliveira's genius in his approach of training was to be able to instinctively know where the position was on each horse to produce what he needed. The quality of the horses that the Mestre chose was not the best ever. Why? Because he liked the difficulty! He liked to figure things out! This was satisfying for him. The puzzle was part of his laboratory.

There was always a sort of competition going on between the Mestre and his friends. The big challenge these trainers liked to pose to themselves and to each other was to take un-gifted horses and train them. I remember

going to Dr. Guilherme Borba's Quinta do Chafariz, just above Póvoa
Santo Adrião, to a big party, where Dr. Borba (who was instrumental
in setting up the Portuguese School of Equestrian Art) showed us his new
horse. The horse came into the *picadeiro* directly from the field, looking
awful! So awful! Everyone laughed and smiled, saying schooling the horse
in dressage would never work—the flying change would be impossible,
he would never piaffe, he couldn't even bend enough to do a shoulder-in…
And then nine months later Dr. Borba would get us all together again,
have another big party, and the horse was completely trained!

So you see it was a friendly competition, but a serious competition: to take
the worst, most ill-suited horse you could imagine and train him to the high
school level. It was entertaining but also beneficial to both horse and rider.

//and sometimes a different method.

Mestre Oliveira had specific horses with specific problems. He dealt
with those one by one. At one point he briefly experimented with a system
that created a head carriage (what we call today a "dumb jockey"). There
were two side reins to put the horse's head down and two reins up higher
so the horse couldn't put his head up or down, resulting in a fixed *ramener*
(positioning of the head and neck). The results were very mixed with ten
or twelve horses. As a result of what I saw—blockage of the neck created
a lot of other problems, like blocking the back or one or other side—I knew
this kind of system was not for me. Perhaps the Mestre was searching
for the miracle, that one thing you can use to put a horse in a position to
accept *everything*.

reflections.

"I have made countless errors
in the training of literally thousands of horses."
Mestre Oliveira wrote
in Reflections on Equestrian Art.

"Luckily, I am aware of these faults,
for otherwise I would never have made further progress.
I know that I still have much to learn,
and will go on learning until my dying day,
not only by riding, but by studying, thinking deeply,
and observing.... More often than not,
it is we ourselves who keep a horse
from performing an exercise correctly,
and classically, by incorrect use of the aids,
and by a poor seat."

MS THAT THE STRONGER

our desire to change something, to "make it happen," the more elusive our power is to do so.

//the circle of friends.

During the first of my two periods of
time in Portugal, I had the occasion to
meet Dom Diogo de Bragança, Dr. Guilherme Borba, Dr. Celestino da Costa,
and the fascinating Senhora Conchita
Cintrón, the first woman allowed to
bullfight in Portugal, all of whom visited Mestre Oliveira in Póvoa de Santo
Adrião. I also visited, with the Mestre,
João Branco Núncio, the renowned
(male) bullfighter, in Alcácer do Sal.

*I believe that Oliveira's genius
in his approach of training
was to be able to instinctively
know where the position
was on each horse
to produce what he needed.
The quality of the horses
that the Mestre chose
was not the best ever.*

The manège at Póvoa de Santo Adrião
was on Dr. Borba's property. In his
private *picadeiro*, up the hill from the
manège of the Mestre, Dr. Borba had
his two great friends, Dom Diogo de
Bragança and Dr. Celestino da Costa,
riding all together. They were all also
students of the Mestre. All three of
these men trained horses to the highest
level. It was a very exclusive club.

Dom Diogo was a man of great
dignity, great refinement, and great

erudition. While all three men had read the major books written about equestrian art in French and German, Dom Diogo had the ability in his own book *L'Équitation de Tradition Française*, not only to translate, but to consider the complete work of François Baucher and *make it understandable on the practical level*.

Dr. Celestino da Costa was a much more accessible personality. He was the older man among the group with a very congenial way. He was a world-renowned heart surgeon and a tremendous rider and trainer.

Dr. Borba was a veterinarian, who, along with a few other friends, had helped Don Alvaro Domecq Romero found the Royal Andalusian School of Equestrian Art in Jerez de la Frontera, Spain. After a very successful start of the school in Spain, in 1979 they decided to create a similar school in Portugal, which was initially mostly students of the Mestre, including Senhor José Athayde, a bullfighter and eventual head of the Coudelaria Alter Real breeding farm, which long served to preserve the Lusitano horse of the Alter Real line. And of course my friend Luis Valença was a founding member of the school, as well.

//the founding of the portuguese school.

As all the participants and the directors of the new Portuguese School of Equestrian Art were students of Mestre Oliveira, there was some uneasiness with the Mestre when it happened. It has been said that the Mestre was offered the position as head of the school but declined. I don't know if this is true. I just know that it was a difficult time for all involved.

▲ *The Mestre in piaffe on Levante along the wall of the picadeiro.*

Dr. Borba made the decision that only Alter Real horses would be used in the school. I do think this was a great mistake as it meant that none of the other important breeders would or could offer their support of the school. The school was then plagued by financial stress its entire existence as it also had little or no support from the government. For many years, it was based at the Sociedade Hípica Portuguesa, Campo Grande, in Lisbon, where a few Alter Real horses were installed and in training. At that time Filipe Graciosa, who would eventually become the Director and *Mestre Picador Chefe*, was a young man. Today the school is undergoing another evolution and while some of its horses remain in the Gardens of the National Palace of Queluz, regular presentations to the public take place in the Henrique Calado Picadeiro, in Calçada da Ajuda, in Lisbon.

Before my time in Portugal, all the gentlemen who were friends and students of the Mestre worked very closely together. Many students from France and Belgium came and visited on a regular basis. During my time, those visits were, sadly, very rare.

//the united states the first time.

Only two months after I had arrived in Póvoa de Santo Adrião and had the tremendous experience with the gray horse in canter, I had the opportunity to go to the United States for the first time. Two students of the Mestre, Patty Favara and her friend, asked me to go and help them in Colorado where they were starting a training barn. I went immediately to the Mestre and spoke directly with him about this. I wanted to stay in Portugal, but as they were clients and friends of the Mestre, I wasn't sure how I should respond to the request.

The Mestre said I should go, but that I must come back. So, I went, reluctantly, with his blessing.

We landed in Virginia, and then Patty and her friend drove me through the United States, stopping at major riding stables throughout the country. It was an instructive trip, illuminating and fascinating. We began with visits to Morven Park in Leesburg, Potomac Horse Center in Maryland, and Meredith Manor Riding School in Waverly, West Virginia. We visited schools and barns in the Midwest where there were Saddlebreds, Standardbreds, and Tennessee Walking Horses. Altogether I was impressed more by the organization and marketing of each establishment than by the riding and instruction. There was a lot of "desensitizing" of horses that was definitely not for me.

Finally we arrived in Conifer, Colorado, and Patty's barn. She wanted to start an equitation school there. It was an unlikely place…at an altitude of 10,000 feet with two feet of snow in the morning and two feet of mud in the afternoon. I lived in a small motel—a *very* small motel (which was a bit of a challenge for the boy who had grown up with a hotel and fancy delicatessen as his home)—and helped Patty in any way that I could. Patty had an interesting thought that horses should be ridden with a bosal and a curb bit at the same time. This did not sit well with me, and so I began to think of what else I might do.

One day we went to Denver, where I met my friend Mary Rose, FBHS (Fellow of the British Horse Society). She was the only professional west of the Mississippi with a school for instructors to achieve their BHS credential. Major John Lynch, from Morven Park International Equestrian

Institute, would come give the accreditation tests. I stayed with Mary at West Hampden Training Stables to help her as she was very busy with clinics in other places. I started to learn about the United States in this way. West Hampden was also where I met Debra, the woman who would become my wife years later, while she was directing the instructor program for Mary.

I was happy to have the opportunity to make many contacts in the United States that proved to be useful when I went back to Portugal. Later, it would become my habit to leave Portugal when the Mestre would leave, generally two or three weeks at a time, and travel to give clinics. The people I met during this — my first trip to the United States — would become the points of connection to the places where my career as a clinician began. ∎

learning
WITH THE MESTRE
– by –

Dany Lahaye

I was lucky to meet Mestre Oliveira very early in my life. I was five years old when my parents took me to the inauguration of the Manège de la Fagne Saint-Remacle in Belgium where we lived at the time. It was on that occasion that I saw the Mestre for the first time.

– Meeting a Centaur –

I remember this event quite well, so forceful was the image that struck me. It was as though I had seen something quite magical—I even had the impression that I had seen the apparition of a unicorn, or of something else quite fantastic. I can still picture this bay horse coming along a diagonal wherein he seemed to fly! It was Mestre Oliveira on Corsario, doing the Spanish trot.

▲ *The book page signed by the Mestre.*

*The Mestre was
a research man, having read
all the treatises on equitation.
He experimented with
all the methods used by
the former masters, adapting
them to each horse
and adding his own personal
touch and experience.*

At the time I had already had a pony for three years, which my grandfather had given me and on which he had given me my first lessons. The Mestre was not, therefore, the first horseman I had seen, but he was *not* an ordinary horseman—he was, to me, a centaur.

My mother, who was a pianist, had already been charmed by this man and his equestrian talent. From that day on, she accompanied me to my lessons with him.

Another event also immediately impressed me—namely, the first time the Mestre spoke to me. We had come to his manège as spectators during a teaching session, and my mother brought a book in which there was a photo of Mestre Oliveira on the horse Euclides. Taking me by the hand, she took me to him to ask him for his autograph. I was very shy and hid behind my mother. He leaned toward me, and looking at me with his huge, all-embracing eyes, asked, "And what is the name of this little one?" I uttered my name, still shrinking and so intimidated by this man, who seemed simultaneously gentle and yet so severe!

Nuno Oliveira intimidated more than one individual! In addition to the respect that he earned due to his knowledge and equestrian competence, he also emanated an aura of authority and had tremendous charisma. Even if unrecognized in a crowd, people would always turn to look at him when he passed by.

When I was thirteen years old, my second riding instructor, Luc Pirick, then Director of the Provincial Breeding and Riding School of Gesves (and eventual author of *L'éducation du cheval de selle*), who was also a pupil of Oliveira, enrolled me in one of the Mestre's courses. Beginning then, I never stopped riding with the Mestre until his death fourteen years later, when I was twenty-seven.

– The Mestre as Teacher –

The first concepts of equitation I learned from my grandfather on my pony. But I received my first "real" lessons in Belgium from a very good teacher, Georges Parotte, who (and I learned this only later), had once ridden with Mestre Oliveira. I am very grateful to this man to whom I largely owe my seat.

So that I could progress more rapidly, my parents then enrolled me at Fagne Saint-Remacle where the Mestre came to teach regularly. One day, my instructor (Luc Pirick) said to me: "Nuno Oliveira will be here next

▲ *Lessons with Mestre Oliveira.*

month, and I have registered you in his course." I replied that I had not yet reached a level of skill to ride with the Mestre, but he insisted. To my great surprise I found myself in the most advanced group of horsemen. I was still quite young at the time, but I remember the slightest details! Certain phrases he used still resonate in my ears. He usually never spoke loudly, and with his Portuguese accent, I was obliged to concentrate very hard. I had to apply myself literally to what he was saying in order to perform as he expected. I was lucky that he never became angry with me. Although he was a very patient man, I did see him angry on occasion—and that could be terrible! The very earth then seemed to tremble!

Mestre Oliveira knew how to encourage me when he observed the slightest results or improvement on my part, all the while pushing for me to proceed farther. I think that he had some affection for me because

▲ *Lessons with Mestre Oliveira.*

I was one of his youngest pupils. He was a wonderful teacher, capable of making equitation seem easy, often giving us explicit images to make us understand better. He also had a great sense of humor. He might embellish his lessons with pertinent and ridiculous commentary. He liked to ridicule those horsemen who took themselves too seriously, yet appreciated those who wanted to learn. To them he gave his knowledge. But to those who thought they knew everything, he merely said, "Fine, you rode well," or even, "Your horse is capable of doing many movements, but unfortunately, he is not *rassemblé* [collected]."

In 1978, my family moved to the southwest of France, near Toulouse, and for a year it was like crossing the desert, so low was the level of equestrianism! I was lucky to meet Geneviève Lehr, a pupil of the Mestre, who took me with her to Portugal. It was then that I understood that studying the art of equitation was the right track for me. Nuno Oliveira taught me everything I know about dressage, and apart from his son João, I never wanted any other teacher.

The equitation of the Mestre was an all-encompassing equestrian philosophy that has never left me. It emphasized respect and love for the horse, and focused on the search for balance—both mental and physical for the horse, as well as for the horseman or horsewoman. This requires considerable mastery of yourself—going beyond pure technique in order to be "in osmosis" (becoming one) with your mount, to "put your mind aside" so that something more subtle—perhaps you could call it your "feel" —awakens and you become capable of anticipating the reactions of your horse. This intensive practice opens a door toward the spiritual, which could, I believe, be compared to the practice of meditation or yoga. It prompted me to ride with my heart in order to feel my horse, thereby putting me into a different state of consciousness.

– The Hardest Lesson –

It seems to me that during the final sessions we had together Mestre Oliveira tried to pass on to me something more: He taught me what was the real *rassemblé* in its lightness and in its balance. During the morning lesson, he ordered me to come to him, saying: "Dany, come here!" I wondered what was going to happen to me. "Why do you ride with the snaffle?" he demanded.

"My horse Almansor is very sensitive," I began, and continuing to mumble, I said that it was out of concern for lightness. He scrutinized me maliciously, then saying, "And why do you ride without your spurs?"

Quite ill at ease, I answered that it was for the same reason. Oliveira smiled, announcing: "This afternoon you will ride with the bridle and spurs."

It was a very difficult lesson, which seemed to me very long and which I shall remember all my life. I entered the manège with the other pupil, sliding to the back as not to attract his attention. But he immediately addressed me with: "Ah, Dany drop the snaffle reins and pick up the bridle reins."

I understood that I was going to have a lesson I would never forget.

The Mestre made me practice halts with the spurs at the walk, trot, and canter, *without* using the hands. I thought I came out of it all quite well, only to discover the session was far from over. He asked me over and over again for halts with the spur, demanding I make it more and more "electric" (charged) and rapid, "Like the bite of an insect!" he insisted, repeatedly saying, "Less hands," although I felt my hands were already almost nonexistent! At the end of an interminable period when he repeated more and more loudly, "Jabs with spurs, less hands!" my horse seethed beneath me, becoming rounder, giving the impression that he was about to explode. Then suddenly he moved his legs, stopped in place, and it was at *this very moment* that I felt I "held" his forehand between my legs and hands, and that he was unbelievably light to the hand.

At that moment, the Mestre made me stop completely and said:
"Aaah! *This* is how one asks a horse for the first beats to piaffe!"

Had he told me that he wanted me to piaffe, I would have tried doing it *without* doing exactly what he wanted to teach me. It was my last lesson with the Mestre, but it will forever guide me in my life as an *écuyere*.

▲ *Lahaye riding with her own personal touch.*

– Following His Path –

After the passing of the Mestre, I thought I would never be able to follow the path I had traced until then since he was no longer there to explain it. I feared I might deviate from it. For years I scrupulously repeated his very gestures and movements, seeking within myself the sensations corresponding to the images that he had left with me.

Thus in my equestrian evolution, I went through different phases. First I learned his technique, taking the Mestre as my model as an absolute reference, which he always is and will be for me.

After his death, I continued on my own, reminding myself constantly of his precious advice, using what he had bequeathed to me — namely to seek within myself answers to the new equestrian problems I faced. I adapted, as he had taught me, the techniques that were appropriate to each horse, and I began "to fly with my own wings."

This is how I trained Duché, the leading stallion on my ranch, but I some-times doubted myself and always asked myself if I had not deviated from the path of the Mestre. The day his son João came to ride my stallion was the fated day when the verdict was going to fall, for João always said what he thought, and in a way, not very diplomatically. But when he swung down from the saddle, my greatest reward came as he put his arms around me and said, "Congratulations! You have certainly retained all his liveliness."

I have trained a number of horses now, and little by little, I have realized that I must not simply try to emulate the Mestre. Instead I must also use my own personal touch. I must develop my own personal way of riding and training my horses. The basic principles taught me by my teacher, as well as the equestrian sensitivity he awakened in me, are what have allowed me to succeed. This is true also with respect to how I teach others in order to transmit his equestrian message, but doing so using my own personal manner.

The most important thing is not the goal, but the path achieving it, which must respect the principles of equestrian philosophy; it's equitation based on the quest for *rassembler* and roundness, achieving it with suppleness and the least amount of aids possible: "Act less but correctly."

The Mestre was a research man, having read all the treatises on equitation. He experimented with all the methods used by the former masters, adapting them to each horse and adding his own personal touch and experience. Up to the end of his life, and especially at the end of his life, his art became so refined to the point that he could achieve the unachievable: he could bring a horse whose own conformation had made collection almost impossible into the utmost *rassembler*.

His riding was above all a complete philosophy. He said that there was no single method, but a method for each and every horse. He taught us how to think and reflect.

The Mestre claimed that he had not invented anything, that *l'Oliveirisme* did not exist. He was not attempting to form his pupils into one mold, but rather tried to develop the right qualities that were proper to each and every one of them, allowing them to grow with their own personalities. (This is surely why none of his pupils teaches in the same manner.)

– Influences –

Mestre Oliveira was greatly inspired by François Baucher, of whom he said one should read between the lines. He flared up against those who insisted that the horse's poll must be the highest point and the face set at the vertical, which to him was not essential, for he felt the ideal position of the horse depended upon his conformation and that might be in front of or behind the vertical. He also said that Baucher practiced the shoulder-in, although he never used that term. Each "Baucheriste" interprets the writing of Baucher in his or her own way, but without a doubt the position of the horses schooled by the Mestre most resemble the engravings representing Baucher on horseback. Bunker, one of the last horses schooled by the Mestre, was completely "Baucher-ized" and was an outstanding illustration of Mestre Oliveira's work.

Finally, I would like to add this: what struck me the most when riding the Mestre's horses was how you could feel the softness of his hands in the sweetness of their mouths. ∎

end of *learning with the* mestre

WE NEED TO LEA

to live with passion and curiosity. We need to learn to embrace change.

The lessons were made up of students who came from all over Europe—mostly from France and some from Belgium. They would come for a few days or weeks at a time. There were very few of us who stayed for a long-term education of months or years. After my first trip to the United States and the clinics I gave there, the Mestre had an influx of American students. And with the arrival of the Americans, things

Mestre Oliveira had a very special life when it came to money. He had a mécène (sponsor) from Belgium who each year would purchase a horse the Mestre had been training for him. The price of the horse was the total of all his expenses for the year: the travel, the vets, the food, the wages, all of it. This was the price.

changed a bit. As is their way, the Portuguese were always very respectful, the French formal and well-mannered…and then came the Americans with their much less formal ways and very open, friendly manner. The Mestre sort of hated it and loved it at the same time.

And then the Americans started to ask questions! This was entirely new! Until this time, as was the respectful custom, we were never

reflections.

The Mestre used to say,
"There is the art and there is the mind."
In other words, there is the art of riding,
and there is the technique of riding.

We need to know enough technique that the physical
does not work against us, but the study and application
of technique should not limit artistic creation.
"What is equestrian art?" he wrote
in *Reflections on Equestrian Art.*
"The perfect understanding
between the rider and his horse."

/ chapter V

the basis
of learning.

You must understand that after hours upon hours of watching in silence as the Mestre rode many different horses, opera always in the background, an enormous amount of knowledge was revealed. The Mestre let his best students find their own way; nonverbal communication is teaching at its best. This "watching" was so powerful that—as I've described to you already—I *was* him when I rode. It was surreal then, yet it has continued to feed me these forty plus years: My riding and teaching has been determined by and inspired by the Mestre. Writing this book made me realize just how vivid and alive the actual memories still are, and I am so grateful for and indebted to the Mestre. I could never have found another teacher like him.

But even in the midst of all the nonverbal communication and silent teaching, there was practice and structure. Most of the movements were treated as exercises, meaning that the walk, the trot, the canter, and so on, each had a specific goal and a purpose. Each was carefully choreographed, practiced, and refined. After an amount of refinement, which was also very planned, the next stage commenced—perhaps the progression to canter or piaffe or passage. These stages were developed and timed, depending on the result of the last stage of training. They were also modified. Lessons were constantly fluid, responding in whatever way offered the horse the best exercise for understanding what was needed at a specific time. Mestre Oliveira was a genius in knowing exactly what each horse needed and when.

On one side you had a very calculated, complex, and precise technique created over years of study and experimentation. But this precision was mixed with the most exquisite tact, with feeling, and with constant mindfulness of what was needed in that moment. This was never discussed openly. But we knew technique was very important to the Mestre. He studied, experienced, and used many different ones. The Mestre—along with his fellow students of equestrian art, Dom Diogo, Professor da Costa, and Dr. Borba—studied and learned by reading the old masters. They practiced with their horses and discussed the different methods. And later the Mestre's friend, French dressage rider Michel Henriquet, added to the conversation (as we can see in his book *30 Years with Master Nuno Oliveira*). And also a close connection in Belgium, Monsieur Laurenty, was part of this group.

//never with force.

We understand that because of how the horse's shoulders are attached to his body (without a collarbone), suppleness and relaxation in the horse plays a fundamental role in how he performs the shoulder-in. The lack of bony articulation means that he is held up and held together by tendon and muscle and ligaments. This is why harmony with the rider plays an essential role here. If the horse feels forced or pushed or threatened in the movement, nothing *con*structive happens and *de*structive things compound themselves: tenseness, nervousness, lack of forward movement, lack of willingness, and lack of trust. Only when true self-carriage is obtained can true lightness be obtained. Do not forget the goal of French riding is *descente de mains et descente de jambes* (lower the hand, lower the leg, or more succinctly, *no* hand and *no* leg!).

The Mestre was such an accomplished artist that he could create all other movements from the shoulder-in. It was fascinating: different for every horse, different from right to left on the same horse, and different from walk to trot. Ever-changing, ever-evolving.

This was how I developed my understanding that horse training must be compassionate and sustainable. We must take the horse into account in every moment, in every movement. What can my horse offer now? What may I ask for and maintain? How can I request it in an empathetic manner so that the training works for him and not against our search for relaxation, self-carriage, lightness, and harmony?

In his book, Mestre Oliveira warned us about position and force:
"Riders most frequently make the mistake of leaning toward the inside.

Amongst other inconveniences, this loads the legs (of the horse) which are under the greatest strain." He continued, "Beware of the so-called 'shoulder-in,' so frequently seen, in which the rider pulls on the inside rein while leaning on the same side, with his leg drawn back to jab the horse with the spur, which forces the poor animal to move laterally while remaining twisted, and which takes all impulsion away from the rider, leading to resistance against the rider."

//he will tell you.

In my own book *Dressage for the New Age*, I tried to simplify the understanding of the lateral movements. These forward-and-sideways movements are performed to improve the quality of the horse's gaits — that is what dressage is all about, improving the purity and quality of the gaits. The movements are not a goal in themselves, merely a technique used to refine, and I might add now, encourage brilliance and self-expression from the horse.

The many different names for the lateral movements can be confusing: shoulder-in, haunches-in, renvers, travers, two-track, half pass, head to the wall, tail to the wall, leg-yielding. To simplify this, we can reduce them all into two movements. First, you have the shoulder-in, which is a very different movement from all the others. The horse is bent around the inside leg of the rider and is moving in the direction *away* from his bend. That is, the horse is bent to the right and is moving to the left in shoulder-in right, and vice versa for shoulder-in left.

I would call all the other movements basic haunches-in. The horse bent to the right and moving to the right is in the haunches-in right.

If the haunches-in is done on a diagonal, it is a half pass. If a wall or fence line is beside, in front of, or behind the horse, it is going to be called something else (*renvers, travers, tête au mur*).

The shoulder-in is fundamental, but it is also very dynamic as we can adapt it to each of our horses at every level in their training. The Mestre would constantly adjust the position of the horse's head and neck, add

Mestre Oliveira
always had a plan
and maintained his focus
with and passion
for each horse through
the horse's entire training
progression. It was
endlessly fascinating
to see a horse evolve,
becoming more brilliant
and expressive,
under his training.

more energy or lower the energy, all to help the horse find his own balance and comfort in his movement. From there, with no resistance, progressively, the gaits were refined. As I have said, the Mestre was instinctively an expert at this. Rarely did he search for the right position. He would almost immediately put a horse in a better position if he sensed resistance. He knew where to put the head to achieve the balance that enabled the horse to continue working in relaxation.

reflections.

I am often asked during clinics,
"How do I know where to position
my horse's head for work in-hand,
and later, for the shoulder-in?"

My answer is always, "He will tell you."
Our horses tell us whether a position is right
in the way they move, the way they breathe,
the way they hold themselves tensely
or let go and relax. We have only to listen!
We have only to improve
our own ability to see, to hear, to feel
(to refine our communication).

//progression.

The very tailored shoulder-in was where all the other movements came from, and the Mestre would change the order of progression as needed. Some counter work was introduced, for example, during the work in-hand, such as counter pirouette to the opposite side, which might be done in a very intense way. By this I mean that there was a lot of positioning of the hindquarters, with haunches-in coming directly from the shoulder-in to attain a greater degree of engagement and mobilization of the hindquarters. (Or not…and then the exercise was recreated, perhaps with a different angle or bend or more or less impulsion).

At some point the Mestre would then prepare the flying changes from a refined counter-canter. To do this, the counter-canter was developed and polished, often with a very adapted head position. Sometimes it was very high, or sometimes very low, whatever was needed for that particular horse and his balance to facilitate the flying change. Sometimes it happened in coordination with very strong half-passes, which were excessive but gave the necessary result for a brief time. I watched the Mestre use two-tempi changes when schooling a horse that found flying changes more difficult on one side than the other.

Most times the changes were started to the outside after a corner. There is a "sweet spot," one stride after the corner, that facilitates the flying change. If the horse changes leads to the outside (toward the fenceline or wall), he stays straight. Afterward, the Mestre would ask for flying changes from the half-pass, then one after the corner, and then one before. Of course, a small *picadeiro* is best for this kind of work. A great, large arena loses the benefit of necessitating bend and roundness in a concentrated space.

The flying change is one exercise, among others, where precise geometry in riding can be a tremendous aid. If you know the pattern, you will feel the stride where it is easiest for your horse to make the flying change. Hand position is also very important before the flying change. Generally, a higher hand creates straightness and will bring the horse's back up underneath you. This facilitates a "clean" flying change (meaning both the front and back leg change canter leads at the same time).

Note: *Too much relaxation is not good for the teaching of flying changes. After training is confirmed, everything can then become more relaxed and enjoyable.*

//very considered practice.

I watched the Mestre, very early on in the training of his horses, introduce a hint of *piaffer* or *ébauche*—by mobilizing the haunches he helped the horse to begin to have the feeling of "sitting" on them…just the suggestion of it. The piaffe and the passage were the result of very long practice of refined shoulder-in and haunches-in to make the back stronger and more supple. The length of time spent on these exercises depended on the strength and mental capacity of each horse. So perhaps "long practice" is not correct. Let me say instead "very considered practice." In other words, new movements were not introduced until the basis for all the movements (shoulder-in and haunches-in) was confirmed and absolutely free of resistance, full of relaxation, with the horse expressive and happy in his movement.

Occasionally the Mestre used the Spanish walk, from the *jambette*, to help one or both shoulders, generally after correct work in collection. This is because in the Spanish walk the horse was in an "open"

{}

▲ *After basic collection was achieved, the Mestre might use Spanish walk or Spanish trot
to help horses that were restricted in the shoulder.*

position—the opposite of collection. Spanish trot was, in a few cases, a way to introduce the beginning of the passage. It also made sure that the basic work in collection had been confirmed and done well prior to attempting the passage.

Mestre Oliveira always had a plan and maintained his focus with and passion for each horse through the horse's entire training progression. It was endlessly fascinating to see a horse evolve, becoming more brilliant and expressive, under his training. But to get the full value of what could be learned, the student had to develop his own ability to focus and deepen his own awareness in order to understand what was happening between the Mestre and the horse. In this way my own self-discipline was strengthened and my understanding of mental connection and molecular exchange between horse and human was defined. ▪

learning

WITH THE MESTRE

– by –

Bettina Drummond

I was both intrigued and delighted, when my friend and colleague
Dominique Barbier spoke with me about writing a piece for this
lovely and special book. When I thought deeply on the influence
Mestre Oliveira had on me, I instantly flashed back to the first moment
of looking up at the elegant bay Harpalo Prince, being flexed in the quiet
morning light, and the sound of the hoof falls in the subsequent, effortless
piaffe. The image of the head of the man, watching the sunrise over his
hills, his back curved and effortlessly following the flow of action under
him, and the graceful doe-eyed Anglo-Arab, collected and free in his own
power. With the horse's mouth forming a cloud of froth around the bits,
his gentle nature quivering in cadence to the release of his every joint, both
partners were supple in mind and completely abandoned to the sensation
of their joining. That vision is as fresh now in my heart and mind as it was
at the very moment of perception.

I suppose the greatest influence was right then and there, in that I was shown the possibility of being the *actual source* of an artistic moment. That possibility was impressed upon me. The creative act was then linked to my personal vision.

– Learning to See the Art –

When I first witnessed the Mestre in such a moment, I was still just a small child. Up until then my experience with and exposure to art had been limited to being taught an appreciation of creativity and brought along in an education that encouraged me to hear and see what was all around me. My parents and stepparents filled their everyday lives with moments to savor art in all forms. Once I had reached about the age of seven, my family encouraged me to listen to and truly hear the thoughts of "made" artists on many topics, especially those who explored self-definition, awareness, and individual perception. But it was not until I saw Nuno Oliveira *live* his art that I was exposed to the possibility that lives within all of us—that of releasing an artistic and individual expression outward with the conviction and power that lies latent within the creative force. Nor had I ever really seen what that creative process entailed, nor had I witnessed the sometimes sorrowful and painful pangs that are part of that kind of search for individual expression.

As a child watching, at first, I was only able to perceive the demanding truth behind Oliveira's mastery of his art. To have an impact on the eyes and ears of a child, things have to ring true and connect in a very quirky way to something already in the young person's imagination. Two things have to come together, really: moments of spontaneous happiness, and a combination of quiet focus and instant combustion that makes the child quite wriggle with delight internally (this latter quality being the sole hallmark of a child's rating system when seeing something precious or beautiful for the first time). Experiencing the first element inspires an over-whelming conviction of truth to which the child bears witness. Experienc-ing the second element helps the child gain an inkling of how powerful forces seemingly tamed by a careless ease of control are the mark of many hours of dedicated practice. Such technical prowess distinguishes an artist of caliber from a mere practitioner.

The feeling of "truth" sensed when perceiving a true artist is like the sen-sation of water flowing through one's fingers or wind across one's face. It is the beacon that one can turn to in the confusion that daily striving often brings. It is that awakened an awareness in me—an awareness that it is possible to embellish each breath of the one life each of us has with art-istry. That creative expression could ennoble the simplest act and brighten the most mundane of daily patterns was a truth that was alive and evolv-ing constantly under my eyes. This eventually grew to a kind of validation of the quality of life I wished for myself.

I did not, at that time, have a notion of learning from Mestre Oliveira how to become an artist. I did not yet have such ambitions. But watching his work, time and time again, brought alive the innate artist in *all* who wit-nessed his genius. For me, it created a door in my small "wraparound" internal world—like the rabbit hole entrance to Alice's Wonderland, I could secretly walk through it at any time. It always led to a unique, sometimes odd, sometimes difficult, but always alive and fun new world. Once the route was established, going through that door brought anything within my imagination to an accessible and translatable place in my mind,

▲ *Bettina Drummond.*

▲ *Drummond on Quemacho.*

▲ *Riding her Quarter Horse stallion Shriner Pour Vous et Moi.*

untrammeled by outside influences and fashions, alone, with the sound of what is true to the horse and pure motion, effortlessly paired with the breath of his body and the breadth of his genius. Oliveira affirmed what horses taught him through his art and dedicated his life to that pursuit, and so, for me, he thus became deserving of the simplest of labels: that of "The" Mestre.

– My Own Path –

Now as I come into my own as an artist and as a woman rider whose interests have diversified, I am very much aware that the influence of great men reverberates throughout one's life. One of the privileges of being a student of a great man is to be buoyed by the wave that was his effort; one of the disadvantages is how I felt I must turn my own talent and vision inward and not merely become a pale shadowy copy of my Mestre's message. Thankfully, I am a female and, as such, the notion that I am aping Oliveira on horseback is as ludicrous as the notion that my love for cello quartets is parallel to his love of opera! (I treasure still his collection of classical recordings that he gifted to me.) Physically, in this art form, one's body has its own feel to express, a look that conveys a particular flow to the horse and the eye that beholds the motion. As an independent rider from a different cultural background from that of my teacher, I had my own path to follow and a story that is only mine to tell, with my own particular passion.

Would I have gotten the notion to pursue equestrian art without the influence of Oliveira? I think so, as I had the great luck of the draw to be raised by persons of taste and artistic leaning, as well as a protected environment that nurtured such thoughts within me. In fact, it would have been somewhat of a disgrace after all that advantage early on not to do so! I lived in a world where such aspirations were accepted as normal—indeed, they were the bar to be measured by—so one might say that I had already been filled with the fruitful soil needed for the seed to have a chance to grow. The struggle that most riders must face in order to get to a place in life to cultivate their art was never mine during my formative years. Of course, it has been difficult at times since, as might be expected when attempting to strengthen one's own convictions and for the creative branches of self-expression not to bend in the gale of disapproval often leveled at those who pursue this art form.

I did not need to affirm too loudly my love of the horse and of equestrian art, as this was reflected in the growing sensitivity in my riding, but this also revealed a tentative expression and an insecure grasp of the whole. I faced the struggle of the burgeoning artist in a "sport world" that now barely accepts that horses are, actually, foremost, a part of the *art world*. To be turned loose into the world of competitive dressage after such careful nurturing in the world of Oliveira—and later on, of the Cadre Noir in Saumur—and find none of the acceptance and enjoyment of any of the training principles I held dear, nor the expression of the *descente de mains* held true, was a flattening blow of staggering proportions to me. It truly had not occurred to me how special the world surrounding Oliveira was in creating an atmosphere dedicated to exchanges between horse and rider guided by free choice and firm belief. Add to that the pettiness of the professionals held in a system that rarely sees beyond its own tunnel vision, and I was cast into crisis throughout my thirties. I came through it, oddly enough, when I lost, for a time, the riding power in my seat. This obliged me to focus on transmitting the teachings that I had learned and to tune in to the perspective of people who had not yet been exposed to that rare world of dressage as art but who were aware of the need for it.

I also realized that my sense of artistry was through sound and was not at all visual, and that the compulsion that Oliveira trained in me to throw myself into the movement of the horse had its roots in the movement of words also. Imagine a full circle: Threading through the motion of horses and the emotion poured into them by Oliveira in his riding was a time when I, at age four, listened to the words of Jean Racine as they were read out loud to me, and enchanted by the sonorous power in the intonation of that French poet of poets, I sat like a mouse. The confluence of the stillness that music and words of great worth demand, as well as the immediacy of physical reaction and exactingly measured feeling. This laid out a path for me as an artist, as well as directing me to fellow artists. *That* is what made my young head snap up and my eyes track Mestre Oliveira that first day on Harpalo Prince. Not the extravagant skill of the rider, not the years of training by the master reflected in the horse's body…it was that simultaneously indefinable and meticulous *sound* that comes from letting feeling pour out of one's art. When, on very good days, I am able to match that with my own instrument, then I know that I have not failed Oliveira as a student. A day when he would have looked at me and smiled, nodding, pronounced: "La, oui, Bettina." The sound of this makes me know, even now when I hear it echo in my mind in the privacy of my own backyard, that *haute école* and its very nature are still well and very much alive in my heart and in my art. And *that* is the never-ending gift of the Mestre to me. ∎

end of *learning with the* mestre

IN MY OWN LIFE, EACH

I have thought I have uncovered something new about myself — about my consciousness —
I have been excited to share it with my horses.

//dom jose.

We visited Coudelaria de Alter do Chão, the royal stud farm, which was managed by a special person, and a student and great friend of the Mestre, named José Athayde.

There I met Freddie Knie and the two brothers Gruss. Freddie Knie was the charismatic leader of the famous Swiss National Circus Knie for half a century, and the Gruss Family were

I specifically remember a horse named Farsista—he was able to piaffer classically, sitting on his haunches, then for his transition to passage, he used to open himself (reverse of collection), passage on the spot, and then move off into a spectacular passage forward. What a sight!

▲ *Ferro of Manuel Veiga for Dom José.*

horsemen, renowned in France for their own circus acts. They had very different styles: on one side, you had a very aristocratic aesthetic, while the brothers were very *manouche* (gypsy), bohemian circus types. We all had a great time together, and in the end I bought Dom José, a horse from the breeding of Manuel Tavares Veiga, without papers, but sweet and gifted, and he moved like a cat. And Freddie Knie, Junior, bought the full brother of José for his wife.

I now, suddenly, had *three* horses at home to train and take care of after the day was finished with the Mestre.

//more horses.

I bought a few more horses for clients in the United States during my time at Mestre Oliveira's: Dom Rossio for my friend Mary Rose (an impressive stallion) and Dom Janela for another client (an Anglo-Arab of excellent quality).

Dom Rossio reminded me very much of Jabute, the Mestre's horse that could only be ridden on the curb. Dom Rossio was a substantial horse that had been a bullfighter. He was a tremendous performer, always light as can be, but he needed to be ridden in a double bridle. He taught Mary Rose a great deal — including the fact that even if you are British, you cannot switch to just a snaffle with some horses! They tell us how they want to be ridden.

Dom Janela (which means "window" in Portuguese) got his name because one day I was walking down the street in a small village, and a horse poked his head out of a window to say hello. A few minutes later I heard a horse coming down the street behind me. Turning, I saw the same horse, this time with the window frame around his neck, and the building he had been in falling down behind him! So I thought, "This horse I have to have!" and I named him Dom Janela.

Both came with me to France and later to the United States.

Dom Juan was a tremendously refined Alter Real horse that I found in Sintra where he was a carriage horse! He was too special and fine for driving up

▲ *Debra Barbier riding Dom José during an exhibition in San Francisco, California.*

reflections.

I've mentioned, it was after six in the evening
when the last lessons were done for the day
that the Mestre would talk to his students
and I would begin to work my own horses.

Sometimes he would check in, coming by the manège to see
what was happening, and often I was there with Pasquale.
As you now know, Mestre Oliveira was a man
of very few words. It was rare that he would say something
about what was happening with an individual horse or rider.
You were left to sit, watch, listen, and learn.
Sometimes there was clarity, sometimes not.
Sometimes he would reinforce the direction
in which you were going with, "Yes, carry on
with the work you are doing." This was very important.
It was the confirmation that was needed.
But he would never tell you
what the direction was to begin with.

and down the immense hills in that resort town…so I talked to the driver…
and exchanged him for a more powerful (and much more suitable) horse.

Dom Juan used to do a "vibrating" Spanish walk. And he would eat from
his lips, he was so delicate! I loved him very much, but I was obliged to
sell him to a very sweet student of the Mestre who lived in Belgium because I could not import him to the United States due to his piroplasmosis
(an often tick-borne disease considered exotic by the United States). The
same was the case for Dom Carlos, an elegant dark bay that I loved very
much. My heart was broken to have to leave them behind. But in the horse
business, the best that we can hope for, insist upon even, is for our horses
to have good homes when we must part with them. And I know they did.

//a visit to belgium.

One day I asked the Mestre when he planned to leave for his next clinics.
He said, "Why are you asking?" I responded that I had to organize my
own clinics whenever he was gone. He seemed surprised by this, so
I explained that I had to pay him for his lessons and I pay to keep my
horses—Dom Pasquale, Dom Jose, and Dom Giovanni—stabled and fed.
I needed to go to the United States and teach to be able to do this.

A bit later, he asked why I simply did not come to Belgium with him.
I was very surprised by the offer and of course accepted immediately.

We went to Monsieur Laurenty's place. He and Madame Laurenty
were very special people, and great friends of the Mestre. He had many
students in Belgium, all very good and committed riders. I was a little shy

visits with friends.

//the parrot of santo eulalia.

Guy and Odile Dorget were very old friends of Mestre Oliveira.
Guy had been the Ambassador of France to Lima, Peru,
and the Dorgets used to organize a clinic in Lima every year
for the Mestre. They were educated, erudite, gentle people.
Guy was a great diplomat and friend of General Charles
De Gaulle. Then the Dorgets retired to Portugal at the Quinta
Santo Eulalia, close to Alcácer do Sal.

Odile was a loving mother and a kind-hearted woman.
Horses were the passion of her life — they owned some

Thoroughbred horses from South America. Everything was beautiful and simple—a contrast to what I knew in Avessada. (Much less every-day drama.)

One evening we went to the stable and heard a voice praying out loud in Spanish, but no one was there. I didn't understand where the voice was coming from! Then we met the ancient parrot from Lima that now lived in the barn and was saying his prayers. Apparently in Lima, each week Guy had tried to give the parrot away. But always Odile went looking for him and brought him back home. She loved him so!

The Mestre's friends were *never* ordinary. He was surrounded by genuine characters and interesting, learned people. I was fortunate to make their acquaintance and to see that life can be filled with wonder, with learning, with humor, and with a healthy dose of eccentricity!

//a special afternoon.

One day in the afternoon the Mestre decided to go to Lisbon to a place where he could watch his old movies—they were super-8 and 8-millimeter films of him riding as a young man…sort of *Campino*-style. *Campinos* are Portugal's cowboys, who work cattle on the backs of Lusitanos, using traditional methods and skills.

We met in the Mestre's favorite restaurant, O Paris, and we ate at his preferred table. Then we went to watch the old movies, which had been made during the time that he would go to Azeitão, a parish in Setúbal, Portugal, taking his saddle on the ferry to get there, and coming home late at night. Mestre Oliveira was riding eighteen and nineteen horses a day during this

▲ *Mestre Oliveira in a thoughtful moment on Euclides.*

time. The restored movies were fascinating! The footage of him as a young man showed a very powerful, very physical style of riding. To be aware of the evolution that had occurred was incredible. I was happy to know him when I did—when the riding was more thoughtful—and well after the time of the riding "laboratory," as our friend Luis Valença described it.

//lunch with senhor veiga.

I remember having lunch with the Veiga father and son at their estate and home of the Manuel Veiga Stud, Quinta da Brôa, just outside of Golegã. Senhor Veiga (Senior) wanted to show the Mestre three horses that he thought the Mestre might like to have. We sat at a table in the center of the plaza area in the Quinta, and during lunch, the *Campinos* rode around us, showing us the horses, bringing by the mares and foals. It was incredibly impressive, and it felt even more so knowing that it was prepared especially in honor of the Mestre's visit.

The Mestre was always extremely cordial with not only the host of the lunch or dinner or visit—or any celebration given in his honor—but with *all* the members of the family and the farm staff. He made certain to visit with everyone, thanking them for the honor of being with them and for showing him the horses. Because he was a man of few words, these occasions could seem somber, but they were always full of dignity and respect.

//fiftieth birthday dinner.

When the Mestre turned fifty, I invited him with his wife Branca, along with Phyllis Field and her mother, to dinner in my little house in Avessada. I borrowed chairs and some other basic things to accommodate all my guests. I prepared all the favorite food and drink of the Mestre: *Leitão* (roasted suckling pig), his preferred wine, the liquor he liked (Jack Daniels), and the best Portuguese brandy to finish! It was a marvelous evening… and it remains strong in my memory.

//a time of closeness.

One period in particular, out of all the time that I was in Portugal, was a period of nine months that was very productive.

▲ The inscription reads: "To my dear friend, colleague, and student, as well as cousin, Luiz, a photo that the current idiots that are infesting the world of riding don't consider to be a classic. My Soante in Spanish Walk and in hand. With a hug, from your old friend, Nuno Oliveira"

/ 1 / *Quinta da Avessada: The Mestre with his wife Branca; his daughter Maria Pureza and her daughter Mariana; his son João, his wife Guida, and their twins Hugo and Conçalo; and Miguel; and his son Miguel, his wife Sue, and their children Sara and Nicolas.*
/ 2 / *Oliveira with his grandson Conçalo.*
/ 3 / *Luis Valença with Garoto.*
/ 4 / *Oliveira with Euclides in Italy.*
/ 5 / *Valença and his wife Luisa at the feira in Santarem.*
/ 6 / *Oliveira with Beau Geste in Italy..*
/ 7 / *Valença with Sultão and family (L to R): Sofia, Senhora Luisa, Luisa, and Filipa.*

Well, Nuno just rang the bell for the groom and said, "You madam, now, you may leave. Perhaps you can go with your bullfighter and learn to do one *banderilla*." He was a man who sometimes could be very aggressive, but in those moments, totally clear. This was a very great quality.

– The Comte –

And one time there was a girl who came with her boyfriend who was a Comte. The fellow was a little self-important because he was a Comte. The first time the Comte rides with Nuno he says, "You know, Mestre, my horses go very well with me. I don't have resistance issues with my horses. But I am interested in your philosophy."

Nuno replied, "Okay, ride the horse then."

One circle in walk...and the horse went a little strangely — tense — but the lesson carried on. Then Nuno said to the Comte, "Come down the center line in walk, please." Again the horse was unbalanced and had lost the rhythm. So Nuno announced, "Now you will stop. Perhaps your horses do not have resistance issues with you, but I do — I cannot watch anymore what you are doing."

And the lesson was over.

Nuno Oliveira developed perseverance over the years in his big laboratory. He remained open to learning and understanding new things about the horse from many sources, always with beginning with the horses themselves, but then branching out to his reading and study.

He never refused any information found to be from the great masters through the centuries. He said that he utilized whatever he needed at a given time with his horses. Each horse would tell him what he needed.

– Professional –

At that time there was a professor who was a good friend of Nuno's: Dr. Celestino da Costa. He was a very important man in medicine. He would come often at the end of the day with Senhor Andrade and other prominent men of the time. I didn't usually stay in the room during their discussions, but one day Dr. da Costa said to me: "Nuno, for me, of all the professionals that I know in my life—in medicine, at the university, in the law—Nuno is the best professional that I know among all of them. Why? Because he does everything that is correct, and if it is not correct, then he will change, but he does it all with a great passion, a great fire to learn and to arrive at the correct way."

For me, this was the greatest thing that Nuno transmitted to others… to the people who were open to receiving it.

In the years of 1978 and 1979 I had my own riding school in Lisbon so I didn't go for lessons each day at Nuno's. Sometimes I talked with him on the phone, but other times I didn't call. Instead, I would just take my car and drive to his place for one hour or two, just to absorb the ambiance. For me it was like when you have many problems in your life and so you go to the church to be quiet or to pray. You sit and absorb this feeling, and afterward you feel better…and sometimes you receive an answer. Your mind becomes clean. You find clarity. This is the biggest gift I received

/ 1 / (L to R) Francisco Bessa de Carvahlo,
    Dom José de Athayde, Luis Valença.
/ 2 / Valença with Lince, during an Apassionata
    performance in 2010..
/ 3 / Valença with Sultão, Royal Equestrian Gala.
/ 4 / Valença with Filipa, Luisa, and Sofia at Centro
    Equestre da Lezíria Grande.
/ 5 / Meeting Princess Diana with the Portuguese School
    of Equestrian Art at Windsor Castle.
/ 6 / Valença, following Dr. Filipe Graciosa during
    a performance of the Portuguese School of Equestrian
    Art at the National Palace of Queluz.
/ 7 / Valença performing in Espactaculo.
/ 8 / Valença at the Royal Equestrian Gala with Nicole
    Uphoff (L) and Luisa Valença (R).

▲ *Valença during a performance with the Portuguese School of Equestrian Art.*

All days, every day, because I train young horses, there are many
moments when the image of Nuno comes to me as I am working.
I think he comes to me as a reminder, because if you read books from
the nineteenth century, those of the great masters, you find that one says
one thing and another says the opposite, and there is basically a big fight,
a big controversy. This makes it very difficult to find agreement when
it comes to how best to train horses. During Nuno's life, especially in the
beginning, this big fight was present, and he was trying to come to grips
with it. But after, as he began to understand what he was learning from
the horses, he began to understand that listening to the horses was

the best way. In addition, he began to incorporate what he learned from life itself in his training: his love of music and his love of art. He applied everything that made life better to the way he trained the horse—all the beauty that is part of our world. This integration brought him much better results, much more satisfaction with his work.

Another thing that is very important and has always stayed with me was his love and commitment to his family. His daughter, his sons, his wife—even with the challenges that he faced from time to time, his responsibility to his family was such a big part of his life. The passion that he had for the horses was the same passion he carried for his family. There were little proofs, little moments that I saw all the time that showed his family was never far from his heart and from his thoughts. He would stop in the middle of a lesson and go to call, to talk a few moments with his son or daughter or wife...and then return to the horses. It was the same, you see? They occupied the same space in his heart.

I considered this a great lesson in my own life, as well. It doesn't matter what your profession is—in other words, it isn't only the case with those who work with horses. I think that if you want to achieve balance in your life, hopefully you will have a grand passion for both your working life *and* your family life. This has been very important to me, and it is something I try to show my students each day. ∎

end of *learning with the* mestre

THE HORSE'S HAPPI

must be the rider's primary concern. Love is unconditional.

departure.

A fter two years in Portugal, it was time for me to depart. For me, it was the time to go. This was after the Carnation Revolution and things were very quiet in Avessada. The Mestre was doing well, and things in general were sort of okay—meaning there was casual chaos rather than the frenetic chaos that often surrounded him. I needed to begin the next phase of my life.

I took my seven stallions from the Mestre's barns and walked them, two by two, into Avessada. I found a place for them to stay with the help of the villagers. The people were so kind to me in those days. They found the stable for me, brought hay and grain, helped me to get a water source. The Mestre called me, then and thereafter, "The Prince of Avessada."

My horses were in standing stalls in the stable in the village, which was good preparation for them when they had to take the train to France. Several weeks later, off we went to the station in Malveira, where I loaded them all onto the train car with no partition—just all the stallions together. They stood side by side, three facing four, with only a big rope in front of them and me in the middle (with a big stick) for the eight-day journey. I had a five-liter bottle of wine, two enormous loaves of bread, and a whole large country ham. So off we went in the train bound for France!

In Spain, and then again in France, I had to change trains because the gauge of the rails was different. I had to take all my stallions off and re-load them each time. I had to search for water and maybe something more to eat for myself, but I was always a little worried because I didn't know exactly when the train was leaving. Really, I should have had several people to help with the trip, but I was all alone. It was an adventure, but not one I wish to repeat.

//the united states via france.

I arrived in the little town of La Jarne, near La Rochelle on the west coast of France. I spent a year there with my horses. They had fared well on the journey considering the difficulty and great change in their experience. A veterinarian from the United States had given me medicine with which to treat my horses for piroplasmosis, for if they tested positive, I would not be able to import them. Five horses did very well and were able to come with me when I was ready to leave. Two of them, Dom Carlos and Dom Juan, tested positive for piroplasmosis, and as I mentioned earlier in this book, had to be left behind in Europe in very good homes. Still, it was heartbreaking.

During my year in France I did well, training horses here and there and teaching students a bit. But I was surprised to find that horses received little attention (except from younger riders). There were not many horses in France at that time that could passage and piaffe—and not just any passage and piaffe, but with brilliance and expression! This seemed to me to be another good reason to go to the United States. It is true that I had clients and clinics waiting, but the

ALL of the Mestre remains with me today. His voice, his posture, his PASSION, is always here with me. It's inside of me and IS me. I am always searching for the oneness, the feel, and the way of being that the Mestre put into the student but that so few people kept—a vibration and purity.

lack of interest for my methods and Oliveira's teachings in France was also a disappointment.

Life in America started with the Mestre's daughter, Maria, who had joined me in France and then enrolled in The Art Institute of Chicago while I was teaching and giving clinics. I settled in Sun Valley, Idaho, and after many wonderful adventures, Maria da Pureza returned to Portugal. In Sun Valley I had an incredible barn built for me by clients. It faced my favorite skiing mountain, Mt. Baldy, and life passed as a few pleasant seasons skiing, fishing, and hunting, and training horses. It was a truly marvelous time.

But the best part was that students and riders in America, both professional and non-professional, were open to and hungry for the knowledge I had gained during my time with the Mestre, as well as the ideas this time had formed within me. It was a time of great joy, mixed always with a little sadness that made me appreciate the gifts I had been given. And it was a time of continued learning with horses. I was on my own, free to succeed or fail, each day, with each horse. And truly, I still look at each day in that way. Every time I see a new horse in a clinic it is a time to learn. A time to feel, to explore, and to discover. Where must the balance be to give the horse comfort and the freedom to express himself? How best can I communicate with this horse, and most importantly, what does he want to tell me?

//what resonates today.

ALL of the Mestre remains with me today. His voice, his posture, his PASSION, is always here with me. It's inside of me and IS me. I am always searching for the oneness, the feel, and the way of *being* that the Mestre put into the student but that so few people kept — a vibration and purity. Other people went other ways, perhaps choosing to compete. Each student took from him what they liked and could use, but did not necessarily keep the purity of it.

I felt it was a kind of intellectual play: how to treat the horse like a chess game. But toward the end, the result was only the great beauty of the horse.

//toward the end.

The last time I saw my Mestre, I was visiting with Debra, my wife. I asked him if I could ride, to have a lesson with him in Avessada. He gave me nice horses, we rode a few, and then the Mestre said, proudly and with a bit of show, "Here we ride with spurs!" He knew very well I had not used spurs for years. He came over and put them on me, while I was mounted, and on Debra, too. They were the very traditional "slide-on" spurs that many Portuguese use. I looked at him and remarked, "Thank you, thank you! What a great honor to have the Mestre putting his own spurs on me!" We always had that sort of back-and-forth repartee.

The last conversation I had face to face with him was before he left Portugal for Australia. I said, "Mestre, I see all these people now ask you questions while you are riding and teaching. So may I ask you a question?"

"Of course, Dominique, you may," he replied.

"What I would really like to know, Mestre, is what is happening between you and the horse."

"That I will never talk about," he said. "It is too personal."

"That is sad," said I, "because this is the only question I have and ever have had."

Afterward, I felt really sad for him. I wanted for him to be able to verbalize the intimate feeling that he had. But in reflection, I don't think it was possible. I was asking too much.

reflections.

Developing a loving partnership with our horse,
one that allows for "co-creation"— combining and renewing our own abilities
with those of our horse in an effort to discover
and share brilliance and light — begins with our intention.

Intention demands that we examine our life, our motives, and our way of being.
My friend Keron Psillas, who helped me write this book and contributed
her wonderful photographs, has a saying: "We photograph as we are."
Well, we ride as we are...we live our life as we are. Becoming aware of who we are
is an ongoing process of refinement, like peeling away the layers of an onion.
And everything we touch in the course of our life reflects
that process — which layer is exposed at any given time.

In my own life, each time I have thought I have uncovered something new
about myself — about my consciousness — I have been excited to share it with my horses.
But I have always discovered that they are already "there."
They are not only helping us to achieve our highest transformation,
they are waiting for us when we arrive at each stop on the journey,
when we negotiate each turn on the path.

DOMINIQUE BARBIER

The same thing happened later when I asked him to write the foreword for my book *Dressage for the New Age*. He immediately agreed. But when I sent him the manuscript, he told me that there were too many things that he felt were different from his methods, and that he couldn't agree to participate. Then, when Jean-Louis Sauvat did his book with the Mestre, *Horse and*

I knew I had to "go and teach" to carry on the mission of my Mestre. I believe I have done this, with the purity he instilled in the teaching, but also in my own way, with the evolution of understanding that the purity we seek is one of connection in love. In love for horses and in love and compassion for all that surrounds us.

Rider: Annotated Sketches, many of the comments that Mestre Oliveira made on the drawings were not only very appropriate, but also similar to so many things I had written in *Dressage for the New Age*. The Mestre said things in the book with Sauvat that he had never said before. It sort of validated all I was thinking and had written. Perhaps reading my book helped create a little bit of an opening for him that allowed him to verbalize the intention in his relationship with horses. I hope so.

I am very proud to say that the Mestre was still my friend when he passed away. He was still very close to Luis Valença, too, certainly…but there was not much space in his life for other people. It was a difficult way to live for him and for all of those around him.

//the gift.

Thinking back, now that I have excavated so much from my life during those years before, during, and just after my time in Portugal with the Mestre, the memory from one very special night comes to me. It was certainly one of the most emotional times I had with the Mestre.

He had invited me to dinner. This was not entirely unusual, but after dinner and dessert he started to talk—it was almost like a speech! He was even more serious than normal in his manner that night. He walked into the next room, which adjoined the dining area, and came back with his exhibition boots and the coat he wore when he gave a legendary performance in London. He said to me, "Wear them with honor, as I did."

I was stunned. Totally in shock. I thanked him, of course, and told him I would rather see him doing more presentations. (It was just after his last presentation in Malveira.) He said no, that he wouldn't be giving any more presentations, and he urged me to take the boots and coat, which I have cherished ever since.

It was not long after this that I left Portugal and took my horses to France, and then the United States. This departure, though emotionally difficult, was for me the right time. I knew I had to "go and teach" to carry on

the mission of my Mestre. I believe I have done this, with the purity
he instilled in the teaching, but also in my own way, with the evolution
of understanding that the purity we seek is one of connection in love.
In love for horses and in love and compassion for all that surrounds us.
The Mestre showed me the power and strength of what a fiercely beautiful
life this can be. I am grateful to him for putting me on the path I have
walked these last forty years. ▪

This is how his fire dissipated the fog of our equestrian world of the twentieth century. When the spark came to touch him, it made him a flame that illuminated his own life, that of his family, and that of his pupils in all their humanity. His was a quest to find perfection without respite.

I would like to share with my rider-friends this sentiment, this strong yet melancholic emotion for an "equestrian musician" who went to his grave without his instrument. We were the happy witnesses of the time when he brought himself harmoniously together with the equestrian world, an experience he lived, and which allowed him to find the path to his essential being. Aristotle used to say: "Do not learn, but experience." This formula can be perfectly applied to you, dear Mestre. As a faithful *écuyer-teacher*, you rode from hill to hill, country to country, as does the sun from season to season. With no rest you frequented princes and mendicants, traversing our green valleys to shed the grains absorbed by your furrow.

The absent one inhabits with his presence since he can no longer be here… there…where he was…where he is always expected. This presence, filled with pain, is all the more difficult since it is the actual negation of his presence. Nonetheless, we are Mestre Oliveira's refuge, his salvation, the "beyond" of his life. It is no longer his memory that we gather; it is the future he would expect from this memory.

We do not think, we apprentice-horsemen, that we are perfect. We follow his example, going up regularly to observe the stars. In this world of appearances, we return to our studies, we strike out everything that is superfluous, straighten everything that is crooked, dispel all opacity, and work by imitation. We think of ourselves first as horsemen who have learned from him the art that fulfills its function. Actually, the horseman who creates himself is not drunk on freedom, but instead knows how to school his horse while keeping his eyes fixed on the un-alterable model of a genius like Nuno Oliveira.

In this sense, Mestre Oliveira, you are the "artisan-artist" par excellence. You knew how to construct your own equitation, making it beautiful in the eyes of us all. You penetrated things by allowing yourself to enter them. You invited us, making a simple sign, to follow our own path and to enter authentically into your equestrian world. Who is not capable of being moved by this generosity?

My dear Mestre, you became this and you knew it. You covered yourself in radiance, without a single obstacle preventing unity, without anything to interfere with your intimacy; you had confidence in yourself. Arise, for we need guides like you. ∎

Dany Lahaye

end OF REMEMBRANCES